MY SUN

POEMS

Nkatha Kabira

authorHOUSE®

AuthorHouse™
1663 Liberty Drive
Bloomington, IN 47403
www.authorhouse.com
Phone: 1 (800) 839-8640

Published by AuthorHouse 10/18/2017

ISBN: 978-1-5462-0621-7 (sc)
ISBN: 978-1-5462-0620-0 (e)

Library of Congress Control Number: 2017913326

CONTENTS

ACKNOWLEDGMENTS

Heartfelt thanks to my family for always believing in me.

Thanks to my mother, Prof. Wanjiku M. Kabira - my mentor, my inspiration, my role model and my biggest fan.

Thanks to my father, Dr. Jackson Kabira, thank you for having faith in me.

Thanks to my sisters:

Wairimu, thank you for being a beacon of hope. Wambui, for your courageous spirit, karambu, for your loving spirit.

And to my brother, muturia, for your inspiring determination and relentless spirit.

Thank you all.

Thank you, lord.

I have found the one whom my soul loves

Song of Songs 3:4

FOR YOUR EYES ONLY

His laughter echoes through the
Heavens…his smile lights
The world, like a bushfire in
Summer…his teeth sparkle
Against the golden rays of the
Sun…
His dark russet eyes
Glint with a warmth that melts
The polar ice…
They shine like two-dew
Covered stones…so
Beseeching like the tiger's…
Full of real appreciation and
Warmth…his lips,
So soft…so tender…
His complexion so chocolate,
So charming…so debonair…
His teeth…a perfect alignment…
So white…so firm…
His movements…full of vivacity,
Full of life and vitality…
Like a bird from a cage…flapping
It's wings for a journey it loves
Beyond doubt…a soothing
Unguent emanates from him…

His name is like perfume poured
Out...so natural...so apt,
His scent so sweet...a fragrance
From the valley of Sharon...
So humble...humility oozes
Out of him...like a natural
Fountain...
So blessed...so gifted...with
Words and a voice from the heavens,
Like an angel he glides through
The day with ease and peace...
He says he's lucky...
But I say...He is
Blessed from the heavens...
Thoughts of him...
A special friend I have.

17th April 2004

LAST NIGHT

I thought of nothing
But you...
I dreamt of no one
But you...
I visualized no one in my
Mind but you...
I fantasized of no one
But you...
I pictured no one
But you...
I imagined me with no one
But you...
I was romanticized by no one
But you...
I thought of you
Kissing me...by the moon
I dreamt of you
Holding me...cuddling
With me...by the fire place,
I visualized you and me
Together...just
Kissing...talking...
Laughing...
Viewing you through
Rose tinted glasses...

Romanticizing…
And these thoughts…
These dreams…
Filled me…
Visions I saw of you
By my side…
I watched the sun rise on
Your face…
I heard the birds singing
And I thought
It was you…
I felt the warmth of the sun
And I knew…
It was your body next to mine
I felt and saw the
Beauty of the rising full moon
And I thought…
I was looking at you
I felt the breeze of the wind
On my skin…
And thought it was you
Coming to kiss me…
Thought I saw two birds together
Whispering to each other…
Cuddling and embracing one another…
Flying as one…
And I knew
There and then that it was we…
But then…
I knew these were thoughts

Just thoughts…castles built in the air
My over imaginative mind's eye…
And woke up.

17TH April 2004

The Little Things About You

I like the way
You look at the day
And marvel at its beauty.

I like the way
You look at the storms of life
And simply send a prayer
To heaven and carry on...

I like the way
You take each day at a time
With so much faith...

I like the way
You're so patient
And always have time for others...

I like the way
You express your dreams
Of a beautiful home, an elegant car
And a blissful life.

I like the way
You talk about the different genres
Of music...your passion

For it and the desire to make
The right symphony...

I like the way
You sparkle and light up
At the sound of your favorite songs...

I like the way
You flow with events
That come your way...
How you deal with people
Making it easy for them ...

It's the little things
About you...that draw me
To you...for this is the joy
That pulls me to you...
I like the way
There are so many things
About you, I LIKE!
Making...time spent together worth it
And the moments cherished.

20th April 2004

THE LITTLE THINGS ABOUT YOU – II

I like the way
You call my name
It's sweet and gentle to my ears…

I like the way
You look at me
Holding my eyes with yours
It's cute and charming…

I like the way
You lift your eyebrow
When we agree or disagree
For it tags at me to come along…

I like the way
You kiss my ear
Reaching my thoughts
Consigning them
To the back of my mind…

I like the way
You kiss me
A thousand words
Across the seven seas
Cannot compare to

The heavenly moment of 'us'…

I like the way
Your lips move
When they meet mine
Like two stars
Falling from the heavens…

I like the way
You hold my hand
The way your fingers
Mesh with mine
Bringing us closer…

I like the way
You hug me
Holding me close to you…

I like the way
Your hand finds its way
Round my waist and
Where your gentle fingers
Find rest…

I like the way
Our steps are in step
It's enchanting…
Like walking on sunshine…

I like the way
The many 'little things'
About you, are endless…
For…
It's the little things about you
That draw me to you.

20th April 2004

ONLY YOU

Only you…
Can make me wake up
To the sounds of the chirping birds
Hoping that you'll call.

Only you…
Can make me rush to the office
And connect to the net
Hoping that there's mail for me.

Only you…
Can make me stare at the phone
When I'm meant to be working
Hoping that you'll call.

Only you …
Can take my thoughts away
And hold my concentration
Hoping that you can feel me.

Only you…
Can make me rush for lunch
And be done with my meal
Hoping that you'll call as you did yesterday.

Only you…
Can make me put my work aside
And write down my thoughts
Hoping that you'll identify with me.

Only you…
Can make me rush home
Just to charge my phone
Hoping that you'll call.

Only you…
Can make me get my skates on
To the computer
Hoping that we'll chat.

Only you…
Can make me miss
Friends…to seventh heaven
Hoping that we'll talk.

Only you…
Can make me go to places
We've been to together
Reminiscing on the times we've been together.

Only you…
Can make me look at the moon
And marvel at the stars
Hoping that an angel is watching over you.

Only you…
Can make me send a prayer to heaven
As deep calls to deep
Hoping…

February 2004

My Sun

The memory
Of your voice…
The visions
Of your body next to mine…
The memory
Of your touch…
The visions
Of heavenly bliss…
The recognition
Of your words…
The memory
Of your gentle whispers…
The dreams
Of your beseeching eyes…
The memory
Of your warmth…
The feelings
Of absolute bliss…
The memory
Of your laughter…
The thoughts
Of our undying love…
The fantasies
Of us laughing…
…Kissing

…Cuddling
…Talking from dusk till dawn
The memory
Of your smile…
The poetry
I dared to write
Of mysteries hitherto unrevealed…
The rivers of tears
Of a divine dawning of truth
I found thee…
He who my soul loved
From the beginning of time…
My Sun.

16th June 2012

THE SUN WILL RISE

Felt like the Sun would never rise
Felt like I would never rise if the Sun never rose
Felt like I would never feel the warmth of the Sun again
Felt like without the Sun there'd be no warmth
Felt like the Sun would never shine
Felt like I would never shine if the Sun never shone
Felt like the Sun held the key to my happiness
Felt like I held the key to the Sun's happiness
Felt like without the Sun there'd be no me
Felt like without me there'd be no Sun
Felt like I needed the Sun to grow
Felt like the Sun needed me to grow
Felt like I abandoned the Sun
Felt like the Sun abandoned me
Felt like the Sun never loved me
Felt like I remembered the Sun loving me
Felt like the Sun never remembered me
Felt like I remembered the Sun remembering me
Felt like I knew the Sun
Felt like the Sun knew me like no other
Felt like I needed the Sun to live

Felt like the Sun needed me to live
Felt like the Sun would not live unless I left
Felt like the Sun would leave unless I lived
Feels like the Sun dares to live when I dare to live.

16th June 2012

TRUE STORY

When I hear your voice
My soul leaps with joy
I feel like your soul is touching mine
When you smile at me
My soul dances
I feel the warmth of the sun
When you hug me
My soul remembers
What it feels like to be home
When you touch me
My soul is tickled
I feel it down to my very being
When you laugh
My soul laughs
I feel the joy way down in my heart
When you kiss me
My soul hears yours
I feel and hear the music of our souls
When you banter with me
My soul banters right back
I feel like my soul wonders why
When you run from me
My soul runs from you
I feel like my soul mirrors yours
When I'm with you

My soul dances
I feel like it's a joyful homecoming
When we're apart
My soul prays for yours
Trusting that heaven is watching over you

19th June 2012

IN MINE EYES

Perfect
Imperfect
Perfectly imperfect
Imperfect perfectly
Perfectly imperfectly perfect
Imperfectly perfectly perfect
Perfectly imperfect in mine eyes
In mine eyes imperfectly imperfect
Imperfectly perfectly perfect in mine eyes
Perfectly imperfectly perfect in mine eyes.

16th August 2011

HIDE-AND-SEEK

hide-and-seek
seek-and-hide.

hide-and-seek. seek-the-hide.
seek-and-hide. hide-the-seek.

hide-and-seek. seek-and-hide. hide-the-seek.
seek-the-hide. hide-the-seek. seek-and-hide.

What are we hiding?
What are we seeking?
What are we hiding from?
What are we seeking for?
What are we hiding to seek?
What are we seeking to hide?
What are we seeking when we hide?
What are we hiding when we seek?
What are we hiding and seeking for?
What are we seeking and hiding from?
What are we seeking to hide when we hide to seek?
What are we hiding to seek when we seek to hide?
What are we seeking to hide when we hide to seek and seek to hide?
What are we hiding to seek when we seek to hide and hide to seek?
What are we seeking to hide when we hide to seek and seek to hide and hide to seek?
What are we hiding to seek when we seek to hide and hide to seek and seek to hide?
Hideandseekandhideandseekandseekandhideandhideandseekandhideandseekandhideevol.

22nd June 2012

21

Chickens

He's chicken
That's what it is
He's chicken
That's what he is
She's chicken
That's what she is
She's chicken
That's what it is
He's chicken
That's who he is
She's chicken
That's who she is
They're both
Just
CHICKENS!

1st September 2012

MUSN'T

musn't forget the pain
musn't forget the hurt
musn't forget the heartbreak
musn't forget the cause
musn't forget the torture
musn't forget the anguish
musn't forget the distress
musn't forget the heartache
musn't forget the anger
musn't forget the tears
musn't forget the shock
musn't forget the horror
musn't repeat the pain
MUSN'T!

18th August 2012

BREAKING FREE

---

tried...
tried breaking these chains
tried and tried
tried fighting the darkness
tried and tried and tried
tried facing the thunder
tried and tried and tried and tried
tried to stop the bleeding
tried and tried and tried and tried and tried
tried freeing myself from the shackles
tried breaking free
tried...
tried breaking this chord
tried but failed
tried crawling away
tried and tried but failed
tried walking away
tried and tried and tried but failed
tried running away
tried and tried and tried and tried but failed
tried setting myself free from it
tried breaking free
no matter what I do
no matter where I go
no matter what I say

I find myself right where I started
on the same path
right where it all begins.

18th September 2012

F R E E

I AM

Breaking through
Remembering
Everlasting love
Awakening
Kneeling and fasting
In prayer
Never forgetting
God is love

Forever
Remembering
Everlasting
Eternal and divine love

By

His Stripes   His Peace   Her Peace   Her Stripes
Her Strength   His Strength
His Love   His Grace   Her Love
Her Grace
His Mercy   Her Faith   His Faith   Her Mercy

I AM

Healed
Ever joyful
Awakened
Loved
Ever grateful
Delivered

By
The Divine Heart of God

I AM FREE.

24th September 2012

I Surrender

My Sun,

I searched for you…

My Sun,

I waited for you…

My Sun,

I dreamed of you…

My Sun,

I looked for you…

My Sun,

I longed for you…

My Sun,

From sunrise to sunset
From moonrise to moonset
From star rise to star set

I searched for you...

My Sun,

I watched the sunrise
I waited for the sun to shine
I longed for your warmth
I yearned for your embrace...

My Sun,

Day after day
Month after month
Year after year
Generation after generation
I looked for you...

My Sun,

I finally found you...

My Sun,

I remembered you...

My sun,

I never forgot you...

My sun,

I never stopped loving you…

My Sun,

I loved you throughout time…

My Sun,

You recalled not our love
You forgot me
You didn't remember me
You abandoned me
You recalled not our sacred pact…

My Sun,

I wept
I was broken
I was crushed
I was in pain—soul pain
I found you only to loose you again
I was confused….shaken and broken.

Did I imagine our love?

No, our love was real…
I remember it vividly
Clearly…it's still crystal clear
Crystal clear…in mine mind.

My sun,
I can still hear the sound of your voice
I can still recall…
The first time I heard your voice,
I recognized it, my Sun…
I knew your voice; I'd heard it before
Like a remembered chord of music…
I knew your voice, my Sun…
Your voice was etched in my heart
Engraved in my memory…never to depart
Your voice beckoned me to an everlasting orchestra
I knew you my Sun, the moment you spoke to me
I knew you…I remembered you

My sun,
I can still recall our first kiss
I can still remember you titled my head to your left
The first time you kissed me
I knew it was not the first
The first time in this lifetime maybe
But you lips, your mouth, your body
We had been together before
It was bliss…
I knew you, my Sun. I knew you.

My Sun,

My heart cried out…
The first time we were locked in passionate embrace
My body jumped out of my spirit and my soul

I felt pain and joy
I felt love and fear
Happiness
Anguish
Bliss
Pain
Heaven
Terror
Joy
I felt like I was home
My sun, I was finally home with he who my soul loved.

My Sun,

The first time when we lay in bed side to side
I knew that there was no place in the world that I'd
rather be

My sun, that day…that day…that cold night in May…
I was home…being in your arms again
Brought tears to my eyes
I could finally feel the warmth of the Sun
My Sun was mine and I was His
Sealed in an eternal covenanted embrace.

My Sun,

The heaven beckoned us
The heavens and skies roared

When you kissed me by the traffic lights
Darkness and lightness befell upon us
The kiss sealed an eternal covenant
A familiar covenant…one we'd made before

My sun, my love…

We'd made this covenant before…
That day…that beautiful sunny day
I looked at you and saw myself
I looked at myself and saw you
You are me and I am you

My sun,

As I look at the sun today,
I know that we are One,
We have always been one
We have never been apart
We were never separated
We loved each other
Throughout the centuries
…the eons…the years
This love is unbreakable
It's eternal
It's divine

My sun,

You are my yin

I am your yang
You are my yang
I am your yin
You are me
I am you
Our love is everlasting
My sun, my love,

Walk your path
My sun, my love,
I will walk my path
My love, my sun,
I believe in you

My sun, my love,

I believe in us
My love, my sun,
I pray for you
My sun, my love,
I pray for us

My sun, my love,

I surrender to God
My sun, my love,
I surrender our love to God
He who knows all things
He whose plan is better and bigger than all things
He who knows what's best for us

He who knows so very well
When
How
Why
We will reunite
He knows us better than we know ourselves
He knows the plans he has for us
He knows the purpose we have alone, together and in
communion with Him
My God,
Our God,
You remember our sacred covenant
You remember our sacred pact
You remember our individual destiny
You remember our collective destiny
For
You know all things
You predestinated us
And
In your perfect perfect time
Your will
Your will
Will be revealed to us
And
Piece by piece
Piece by piece
I will remember Who I am
He will remember Who He is
We will remember Who We are
I will remember Why I am Here

He will remember Why He is Here
We will remember why we are here

And

We will remember to whom we belong

I SURRENDER

To God's divine and perfect plan.

14th August 2012

BORN TO SHINE

The sun rose
In a little village
One morning in March
Before the fishermen set out sails
Women ululating
Outside a lowly hut
Little boy born
Unto us a baby boy born
Born to rise with the sun
Born to shine
Born to bring warmth to the world
Born to light up the world
light up the skies
light up our lives
Born to be different
Born to go against the grain
Born to dare to be
Born to live
Born to love
Little boy born
When the sun shone
The son of the sun
The father of the sun
The daughter of the sun
The mother of the sun

Unto us a baby boy born
Born to bring sunshine
Born to dream
Born to dare
Born to discover
Born to deliver
Born to heal
Born to envision
Born to teach
Born to encourage
Born to love
Born to love to love
Little boy born
When the sun shone…
I bear with me news
I bring with me great tidings
I have a message for you
a message from up above
You were born to bring warmth
You were born with a yearning
You were born with a yearning to question
You were born with the answers
You were born to unravel mysteries
You were born to discover the truth
You were born to share your truth
You were born to share universal truths
You were born to share our truths
You are here for me
You are here for us
You carry with you a message from God

You carry a message from the divine
…a message of love
…a message of light
…a message of truth
Little boy born
When the sun shone…
Unto us a baby boy born
Born to the sun
Born of the sun
Born for the sun
Born from the sun
Born with the sun
Born when the sun shone
Son of the sun
Daughter of the sun
Mother of the sun
Father of the sun
You bear a message for all humanity
…a message of love
…a message of light
…a message of truth
You are here for me
You are here for us
You are here for all humanity.
Dare to be, my Sun!
DARE TO BE!
You were born to love.
You were born to shine.

22nd August 2012

SHIMMER AND SHINE

Shimmering
Shining
Sparkling
Glimmering
Glowing
Gleaming
It's a heavenly sign...
The sun is rising!
Shining Shimmering
Shimmering Shining
Sparkling Shimmering
Glimmering Glowing
Glowing Gleaming
Gleaming Glimmering
It's a heavenly sign...
The sun is shining!
Shining Shimmering Glimmering
Shimmering Shining Glowing
Sparkling Shimmering Gleaming
Glimmering Glowing Shining
Glowing Gleaming Shimmering
Gleaming Glimmering Sparkling
It's a heavenly sign...
The sun is here!
Shimmer and Shine

Glimmer and Glow
Sparkle and Twinkle
Gleamer and Shine
Sparkle and Twinkle
The heavens awaken…
Unto us…
The sun is born.

22nd August 2012

Pure Love

Dear Lord,
Liken me to you
Your graciousness
Your lovingness
Your kindness
Your gentleness
Your forgiveness
Your thoughtfulness

Dear Lord,
Liken me to you
Your strength
Your patience
Your compassion
Your courage
Your faith
Your mercy

Dear Lord,
Liken me to you
Your loving-kindness
Your loving-graciousness
Your loving-gentleness
Your loving-patience
Your loving-forgiveness

Your loving-thoughtfulness

Dear Lord,
Liken me to you
As you say in your word
You are the potter and I am the clay
I belong to you
I am your daughter, your child
And I want to see you smile
I want to love you the way you love me
More and more
I want to love you

Dear Lord,
Liken me to you
I feel your presence in my life
I experience your grace everyday in my life
I don't always see it –I'm sorry
Every single day of my life
You are walking the path with me
I know you are
The songs in my heart
Remind me of your presence
I sometimes forget- I'm sorry
But I know you are there with me
I sing because you sing
Every step of the way
You are right there

Dear Lord,
Liken me to you
I love you for all
I thank you for all
With all that is within me
With all that I have
With all that I am
I'll seek your face
I'll see your smile
I'll chase after you
I thank you for never letting me forget you
And your love for me

Dear Lord,
Please, make me like you
I need you
More and more
I need you
Lord, make me like you
Mould me and create in me anew
Lord, mold your daughter into love
Like You, Lord. Like You.
Pure love.
Amen.

11th October 2012

[N]EVER

Never
Ever
Never
Ever
Never
Ever
Ever
Never
Never
Ever
Never
Never
Ever
Ever
Never Ever
Never Never
Never Never Ever
Never Never Never Ever
Never Ever Say Never
Ever Never Say Ever
Never Never Ever Say Never
Never Ever Never Say Never
If Ever Never Ever Say Never

Then Never Ever Never say Never
For Never is Ever Never Ever Never
And Never is Never Never Ever Never.

11th October 2011

A LITTLE CONVERSATION WITH GOD

Dear God,

> It's me.

> It's me, again.

> You know, your daughter?

Yes.

> Your daughter from Africa?

Yes. Yes.

> Your daughter from the far south...You know- where Nyambene Hills sing to you; where Mr. Kenya stands majestic; where the winds blow in your face; where the rivers run deep; where the valleys and the rocks cry out to you; and where the skies are bluer than blueberries

and truer than truly lovely;
o what a blessing.

I can't sleep!

Why do you keep waking me
up? I have work to do in the
morning.

Why, Lord? Why?
And in the middle of the
night- in the dead of night?

Because...

                    Because, what?

You are too busy during the day to hear me.

I keep calling out your name
And you don't answer.
                    Ok, I'm up now.
                    Speak
                    Speak, Lord. I'm
                    listening.

I just woke you up to tell you

I love you

You woketh me up to tell me
that you loveth me?

As in, seriously?
Yes, I love you my daughter
Just the way you are
You are fearfully and wonderfully made.
You are love.
You, my daughter, are love.
Now, go back to bed.

I love you too, Lord
Goodnight.

11th October 2012

HARD TO IMAGINE

It's hard to imagine that
I imagined it all
It's hard to imagine that
It was all- just but a dream
It's hard to imagine that
He doesn't care
It's hard to imagine that
He doesn't love me
It's hard to imagine that
He doesn't know me
It's hard to imagine that
He doesn't remember me
It's hard to imagine that
He forgot all about me
It's hard to imagine that
He gave up on us
It's hard to imagine that
He is living his life and doesn't care
It's hard to imagine that
He is moving on without me
It's hard to imagine that
He left and is never coming back
It's hard to imagine that
He chose to love another
It's hard to imagine that

He might never return
It's hard to imagine that
He never felt the way I did
It's hard to imagine that
He erased all the memories of us
It's hard to imagine that
He gave up on the dream
It's hard to imagine that
He chose to leave
It's hard to imagine that
He abandoned the plan
It's hard to imagine that
He chose to abandon me
It's hard to imagine that
He never truly knew me
It's hard to imagine that
He misunderstood me
It's hard to imagine that
He chose not to truly hear me
It's hard to imagine that
He wasn't my true love after all
It's hard to imagine that
He wasn't who I thought he was
It's hard to imagine that
He wasn't the Sun
It's hard to imagine that
He was unkind to me
It's hard to imagine that
He annoyed me on purpose
It's hard to imagine that

He let me go
It's hard to imagine that
He never tried to find me again
It's hard to imagine that
He never missed me
It's hard to imagine that
He never wanted to see me again
It's hard to imagine that
He never wanted to hear me laugh again
It's hard to imagine that
He never wanted to hold me in his arms again
It's hard to imagine that
He never wanted to make me his
It's hard to imagine that
He wasn't afraid to lose me to another
It's hard to imagine that
He set me free
It's hard to imagine that
He never even tried to find out how I was
It's hard to imagine that
He chose to live his life without me
It's hard to imagine that
He never looked back
It's hard to imagine that
He never felt what I felt
It's hard to imagine that
He took me for granted
It's hard to imagine that
He chose to leave
It's hard to imagine that

He hurt me on purpose
It's hard to imagine that
He never did love me
It's hard to imagine that
He never was
It's hard to imagine that
He never existed
It's hard to imagine that
He never happened
It's hard to imagine that
I imagined it all
Imagine
Imagining
An Imagine-less life?
Imagine
Imagining
A life without imagination?
Imagine
Dis-imagining
When you were created to imagine?
Imagine
Un-imagining
When you imagine to create?
And you create to imagine?
And you create imagining?
And you imagine creating?
And you are a creation of imagination?
And you are an imagination of creation?
It's hard to imagine
Dis-membering from your being

It's hard to imagine
Un-imaging a knowing that rests so firmly within
It's hard to imagine
Re-writing what your heart says to your imagination
It's hard to imagine
Recreating what your mind says to your imagination
It's hard to imagine
Reinventing what you soul says to your imagination
It's hard to imagine
Rethinking what your body says to your imagination
It's hard to imagine
Re-imagining a reality that isn't so
It's hard to imagine
Rewriting a dream sans imagination
It's hard to imagine
Rewriting your imagination sans the dream
It's just so hard imagining when it goes against
What your imagination is truly saying
To live imagining
To imagine living
To choose to re-member and remember
To never stop imagining love
To never stop imagining hope
To never stop believing in the power of imagination
The secrets to my souls lie therein
In my imagination
That's why I live
That's how I live
That's why I love
And choose love to live

And live to choose love
I live to imagine
I imagine to live
I live to imagine love
I love to imagine
I love to imagine love.

4th November 2012

THE ULTIMATE SOURCE

Behind the rain
There may be
A thousand rainbows
And one- just one
Is finding its way to me
My heart's unaware
A sweet miracle could happen
Cold, fearful, dejected
Life feels small
Just like the falling rain
Just like the stars in the late-night sky
Life is a beautiful journey
A journey that oft' feels like a cold and hopeless jumble
With no where else to go
I call on God
In stillness…I talk to God
As I listen to the rhythm of the falling rain,
The most beautiful conversation through song ensues
With the voices of the mountains
And the whistling birds
Angelic duets –we make
With the choirs in heaven
The most beautiful sounds are born
All of a sudden
There's a magical feeling

Deep inside of me
I can't explain
It's unfathomable…a divine feeling
A feeling so strong and true
Behind that sacred place
That cannot be broken
And will not be shaken
Through song, stillness and reflection
I realize the world is not –
Such a hopeless jumble
After all…
Every single day of our lives
God showers us with His blessings
He is the reason for the sunny smiles in the world today
I love the rain
It reminds me of how deep and wide God's love is
Compareth not God's love
For there are no comparables
It's higher and further and higher and further than the furthest stars
It's deeper and wider and wider and deeper than the lakes, oceans and rivers
It's taller and taller and taller and taller than the tallest trees
Make no mistake
He is the ultimate source of it all
He is the ultimate power- the ruler of the universe
He is the ultimate creator- the mover and shaker
In stillness
In song

In prayer
I find peace
You know that feeling?
That feeling of the stars being aligned?
And the world being born anew
That's exactly what it feels like
…the stars, the sun, the moon
…the birds in the skies, the seas
…the mountains, the hills, the lakes
…the oceans, the humming bees, the rainbows
all stills to listen to God
My heart cries out
Tears of joy and happiness
Suddenly, I am reminded of His word
That He will never leave me
That I am never alone
That He loves me O so much
Even when I feel fearful, cold and dejected;
He is always there to carry me under His wings
O how I love Him
I'm in love with the ultimate source
-The giver of life
-The all-powerful creator of the universe
-The one who lights up the shadows
Whenever the darkness and fear tries to follow me
- He who brings me air so I can breath
- He who brings me breath so I can live another day
- He who makes everything new
- He who who makes everything beautiful and o so
wonderful

\- He who –O so loves me from the depths of depths
O how great is thy seed
O how powerful is thy name
O how deep is thy love
O how sweet are thy miracles
You are the ultimate source.

28th November 2012

BEFORE
I LOVED YOU
(I LOVED YOU)

Before
    I met you
        (I loved you)
           Before
           I loved you
               (I met you)

Before
    I met you
        (I knew you)
           Before
           I knew you
               (I remembered you)

Before
    I remembered you
        (I heard you)
           Before
           I heard you
               (I felt you)

BEFORE
I LOVED YOU
(I LOVED YOU)

Before

    I felt you

        (I saw you)

           Before

              I saw you

                (I felt your touch)

Before

    I felt your touch

        (I knew your touch)

           Before

              I knew your touch

                (I knew you)

Before

    I knew who you were

        (I spoke to you)

           Before

              I spoke to you

                (I knew you)

BEFORE
I LOVED YOU
(I LOVED YOU)

I loved you

    Before

        I met you

            I met you

                Before

                    I loved you

I loved you

    Before

        I knew you

            Before

                I knew you

                    I loved you

I loved you

    Before

        I loved you

            Before

                I loved you

                I loved you.

25th November 2012

AFRICA

When he speaks of Africa

He speaks of She

She of Him

He of Her

When She Speaks of He

When he writes of Africa

He writes of She

She of Him

He of Her

When he writes of Him

When he thinks of Africa

He thinks of She

She of Him

He of Her

When She thinks of He

        When he dreams of Africa

        He dreams of She

        She of Him

        He of Her

        She dreams of Him

When he longs for Africa

He longs for She

She for him

And he for She

She longs for him

Africa

His Africa

Her Africa

Africa

2nd February 2016

WHAT TOOK YOU SO LONG?

I'm waiting…
Your lady-in-waiting is waiting …
What is taking you so long?
Seconds to Minutes
Minutes to Hours
Hours to Days
Days to Weeks
Weeks to Months
Months to Years
I'm waiting…
Your lady-in-waiting awaits …
What takes you so long?
Year after Year
Decade after decade
Century after Century
Millennium after Millennium
Generation after Generation
Eons to Eons
Where art thou?
I'm waiting…
Your lady-in-waiting gets weary awaiting…
What is taking you so long?
Why so long?

17th August 2012

Come Home

When are we going to be together again, my love?
I've prepared a meal- a very special meal
I've prepared the gardens-the beautiful blossoming gardens
When are we going to be in each other's embrace again, my love?
I want to take care of you—to love you
I want things to be the way they were
I want to be in your arms
I want to hold you in my arms and never let you go
When will I see you again, my love?
I've prepared a banquet- a very special banquet
I've prepared a feast- a feast so grand—just the way you always liked it
I've been waiting for you, my love
I've cleared up the granaries
I'm ready for you
I've been prepared for you
When are you coming home?
I'm ready for you
I'm prepared for you
Come home, my love
Come home!

15th August 2012

ABOUT THE AUTHOR

Dr Nkatha Kabira is a Lecturer at the University of Nairobi, School of Law and a postdoctoral W.E.B. Du Bois, Hutchins Fellow at Harvard University. She completed her doctoral degree at Harvard Law School in May 2015. She has professional and research experience in several areas ranging from law and language to security sector governance and to gender and the law. She lectures widely and has taught extensively both in Nairobi and at Harvard and has received awards in recognition of excellence in teaching. Prior to completing the LL.M. Program at HLS in 2008, she worked as a legal associate and pupil at Kaplan and Stratton Advocates in Nairobi, Kenya. She has worked as a research fellow at the Kenya National Commission on Human Rights, the Kenya Law Reform Commission and the Constitution of Kenya Review Commission. She holds a Bachelor of Laws degree from the University of Nairobi and a postgraduate diploma in legal practice from the Kenya School of Law. She is an Advocate of the High Court of Kenya. This is her first book of poetry.

Printed in the United States
By Bookmasters